Cinderhill Bridge on a restored section of the Chesterfield Canal at Shireoaks. This red-brick bridge is typical of the type found on this old canal.

The Architecture of Canals

Derek Pratt

A Shire book

Published in 2005 by Shire Publications Ltd,
Cromwell House, Church Street, Princes Risborough,
Buckinghamshire HP27 9AA, UK.
(Website: www.shirebooks.co.uk)

Copyright © 2005 by Derek Pratt.
First published 2005.
Shire Album 444. ISBN 0 7478 0632 2.
Derek Pratt is hereby identified as the author of this work
in accordance with Section 77 of the Copyright, Designs
and Patents Act 1988.

British Library Cataloguing in Publication Data:
Pratt, Derek
The architecture of canals. – (Shire album; 444)
1. Canals – Great Britain – History
2. Hydraulic structures – Great Britain – History
3. Industrial buildings – Great Britain – History
I. Title 627.1'3'0941
ISBN-10: 0 7478 0632 2

Photography by the author.

Cover: *Grove Park Bridge on the Grand Union Canal near Watford was built in a decorative style to appease the local lord of the manor.*

Printed in Malta by Gutenberg Press Limited, Gudja Road, Tarxien PLA 19, Malta.

Contents

For most of the twentieth century public access to the canals of central Birmingham was not encouraged, but after the massive regeneration programme that began in the 1970s the towpaths were officially opened up to the public. Saturday Bridge is part of a designated waterside walk.

The sinuous lines of Great Haywood Junction Bridge near Stafford. This brick bridge is at the junction of two Brindley-built canals: the Trent & Mersey and the Staffordshire & Worcestershire.

Introduction

The original purpose of canals was to link regions of industry to major rivers and ports. In Britain Birmingham, the Black Country and the Potteries were examples of developing industrial areas where no smooth and safe transport for finished goods was available. In addition there was difficulty in acquiring the bulky raw materials necessary for production when rutted roads and packhorses were the only method of transport. The invention of the pound lock made it possible for water to climb over hills by means of an artificial waterway. The first canals often followed the contours of the land, resorting to locks only when absolutely necessary. Indigenous materials were used to build bridges and soon these early canals blended into the landscape, looking more like a natural feature than a man-made structure. As trade increased, these meandering waterways became impractical and time-consuming. Later canals like the Birmingham & Liverpool Junction Canal (now the Shropshire Union) were built in a straight line with long flights of locks, deep cuttings and embankments. The impact at the time must have been similar to the construction of today's motorways.

Bromford Junction sign on the Birmingham Canal Navigations.

The pioneer of all canal engineers was James Brindley (1716–72). A former millwright with little education, he became engineer for the Bridgewater Canal (1761) and then progressed to complete his Grand Cross of canals that connected the rivers Trent, Mersey, Severn and Thames. The Trent & Mersey Canal, the Staffordshire & Worcestershire Canal and the Coventry and Oxford Canals remain navigable today and rank high among Britain's most popular cruising waterways. Later engineers such as William Jessop, John Rennie, Benjamin Outram and Thomas Telford all left their watery signatures on the map of Britain with canals that are still in use and enjoyed by boaters today.

One must not forget the men who actually did the work of digging the canals. Thousands of itinerant labourers, known as 'navvies', worked with pick, shovel and wheelbarrow. Bricklayers, stonemasons, carpenters and blacksmiths were among the thousands of skilled craftsmen needed to build locks, tunnels, aqueducts, bridges and embankments. Surveying methods were primitive and accidents to workers were common, especially in difficult weather conditions. Together the engineers, skilled craftsmen and labourers constructed a network of canals that have stood the test of time.

Bridges

Bridges were originally built to cross over rivers, replacing fords or primitive stepping stones. In Britain clapper bridges provided one of the earliest types of river crossing. These raised stone slabs allowed water to pass underneath while being broad enough to support people and horses. Examples of these can still be found at Postbridge in Devon and Tarr Steps in Somerset. Fine examples of medieval bridges can be seen at many places throughout Britain, and bridge-building had progressed to a fine art by the time the canals made their appearance in the latter part of the eighteenth century.

On the early canals bridges tended to be built in brick or stone – whichever material was readily available in the locality. During the later period of canal construction the use of cast iron became prominent in the building of canal bridges. The engineer responsible for building a particular section would appoint a local builder to erect a number of bridges. These local builders often left a mark or a particular flourish as an individual signature for posterity.

An electrically operated lift bridge at Aldermaston on the Kennet & Avon Canal. This bridge carries the canal across a main road where traffic is controlled by lights.

Canals are usually narrower than rivers, so canal bridges are almost always single-arched. When it was too expensive or inconvenient to build high arched bridges a compromise was found by constructing lifting bridges on narrow canals and swing bridges on broader canals, thereby avoiding the problem of headroom for boats and barges. Excellent examples of lifting

This swing bridge, carrying a busy road over the Leeds & Liverpool Canal at East Riddlesden near Keighley in West Yorkshire, is electrically operated. Swing bridges usually pivot on a turntable and manually operated ones are often hard work to move.

bridges can be seen on the Oxford and Llangollen Canals. Swing bridges are common on the Leeds & Liverpool Canal, especially on the Yorkshire section, and can also be found on the Kennet & Avon Canal. Electrically powered swing bridges or lifting bridges are used when they impinge on a road crossing. In this case speed of operation is important when a queue of impatient motorists is waiting behind the barriers. In places where the bridges merely provide a crossing for farm vehicles, they have to be moved manually.

A manually operated lift bridge on the Prees Arm of the Llangollen Canal. Bridges of this type are usually pedestrian or farming accommodation bridges.

One of the best examples of a 'snake' bridge is this one at Congleton on the Macclesfield Canal. The convolutions of this stone-built bridge allowed the boathorse to cross the canal without being unhitched.

In the early days of the canals all boats were horse-drawn and, if the towpath changed sides, there was a problem in getting the horse over the canal without unhitching it from the boat. Some canal engineers solved this in ingenious ways. The snake bridges on the Macclesfield Canal allow the horse to walk up an exaggerated stone ramp that curls around in a tight spiral to another ramp on the opposite side. On the Stratford-upon-Avon Canal, the cast-iron bridges were built with a split through the decking so that the towrope could be passed through.

Some of the finest bridges can be seen where a canal passed through land once belonging to the gentry. After agreeing

A split bridge on the Stratford-upon-Avon Canal at Lapworth. It enabled the boathorse's rope to be passed through without unhitching. Two cast-iron cantilevered sections leave a small gap. This is a much simpler and cheaper method of achieving the same result as the 'snake' bridges on the Macclesfield Canal.

A section of the balustraded Lady's Bridge on the Kennet & Avon Canal near Wilcot.

Below: Cast-iron Horseley Iron Works bridges at Windmill End on the Dudley Canal. The derelict Cobb's engine house can be seen in the background.

to allow the canal to be built across his land, his lordship often stipulated that the crossing bridges should be highly decorative. Examples of such canal bridges can be seen at Grove Park near Watford on the Grand Union Canal, Avenue Bridge near Brewood on the Shropshire Union Canal and Lady's Bridge near Wilcot on the Kennet & Avon Canal.

Cast-iron bridges are often very elegant structures, especially those constructed in the Black Country by the Horseley Iron Works. These are found extensively on the Birmingham and Black Country canals and also further south on the Oxford Canal. There is one excellent cast-iron turnover bridge as far south as Osterley near Brentford on the southern

A cast-iron Horseley Iron Works bridge at Rugby Wharf on the north Oxford Canal. This type of bridge normally carries the towpath over a canal junction or a canal arm.

The double-arched junction bridge at Braunston Turn is made of cast iron with brick abutments. This is the junction of the Grand Union and Oxford Canals.

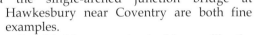

Grand Union Canal. Cast iron is sometimes used on pedestrian turnover bridges, where the towpath changes sides, and also on junction bridges. The twin-arched cast-iron junction bridge at Braunston and the single-arched junction bridge at Hawkesbury near Coventry are both fine examples.

Canal bridges can also be bizarre, like the Locomotive Bridge at Huddersfield, which looks as if it was constructed from giant Meccano pieces. The outrageous folly bridge at Drayton Bassett on the Birmingham & Fazeley Canal has fortress-like towers, each with an internal spiral staircase to enable pedestrians to cross the canal on a walkway. An adjacent swing bridge makes the whole concept redundant except, of course, when a boat passes through.

In the days of horse-drawn boats, the constant chafing of taut wet towropes caused deep grooves in the bridge's brick or

Constant rubbing by taut wet towropes coated with dirt has eaten into the stonework of this bridge at Burnley on the Leeds & Liverpool Canal. Rope chafing can be seen on bridges all over the canal system and provides a fascinating insight into the generations of boatmen and their horses who once toiled along the towpaths.

Stonemasons restoring a bridge at Bugsworth Basin on the Upper Peak Forest Canal.

Gailey Bridge plate, Staffordshire & Worcestershire Canal.

stonework. Iron bridge plates were introduced to protect the structures but eventually even they were grooved by the ropes.

In Regent's Park, London, Macclesfield Bridge spans a shallow cutting near London Zoo. In October 1874 a barge containing gunpowder blew up directly underneath the bridge, destroying the bridge, the boat and its occupants. The bridge was eventually rebuilt using the original supporting columns, which were re-erected facing the wrong way. The result is a set of grooves on one side made before the explosion and a set made in the years afterwards. The bridge has achieved lasting fame as 'Blow-up Bridge'.

The construction of modern motorways over existing canals has resulted in a number of prosaic concrete slab bridges, which have little architectural or aesthetic merit. Much more appealing are modern steel footbridges like those at Castlefield in the centre of Manchester and at Apsley on the Grand Union Canal. The huge development at Paddington in London has a unique helix footbridge that rotates and retracts on a steel corkscrew when a boat passes through.

Aqueducts

Canal aqueducts were originally built to span a wide river or river valley. In later years aqueducts crossed railways, roads and, in some cases, other canals.

In 1761 the first aqueduct built for navigation in Britain carried the Bridgewater Canal over the River Irwell at Barton. This remained in place until 1894, when it was demolished during the building of the Manchester Ship Canal. It was replaced by the Barton Swing Aqueduct, a unique structure that swivels to allow ships to pass by.

Many of the earliest aqueducts were squat, inelegant structures such as the Brindley aqueducts carrying the Staffordshire & Worcestershire Canal at Great Haywood and Tixall near Stafford. Later aqueducts, especially those designed by the engineer John Rennie, were built in the classical style with balustrades, columns and other embellishments. Rennie's aqueduct on the Lancaster Canal is a magnificent structure

The unique Barton Swing Aqueduct carries the Bridgewater Canal over the Manchester Ship Canal. It replaced an earlier Brindley aqueduct that was demolished when the Ship Canal was built in 1893. When a large vessel passes along the Ship Canal, the aqueduct swings out of the way.

The Sow Aqueduct on the Staffordshire & Worcestershire Canal near Stafford is a typical low-arched Brindley structure. It occupies a picturesque position on the edge of the wooded Cannock Chase.

built on five arches, 60 feet above the River Lune just north of Lancaster. Rennie's Dundas Aqueduct is designed in classical style and built in Bath stone. Dundas, like its neighbour at Avoncliff, carries the Kennet & Avon Canal over the River Avon. Both aqueducts have needed extensive repairs because of the weathering of the original stone, which has been replaced by better quality stone.

One of the most important aqueducts in the history of canal building still stands forlorn in a field in Shropshire. The Longdon upon Tern Aqueduct once supported the now derelict Shrewsbury Canal. This was Thomas Telford's prototype iron

Built in golden Bath stone, Rennie's Dundas Aqueduct carries the Kennet & Avon Canal over the River Avon on a single arch. For embellishment it has decorated cornices and balustrades.

trough aqueduct that eventually led to the masterpiece of Pontcysyllte. The Pontcysyllte Aqueduct was built to carry the Ellesmere Canal (now called the Llangollen Canal) across the valley of the River Dee near Llangollen. Nineteen masonry arches support an iron trough that carries the canal at a dizzy height of 125 feet above the river valley. It is 1008 feet long and has a towpath protected by a cast-iron railing. The other side of the trough is completely unprotected, leaving only a few inches of iron between the boat and a yawning drop below. Rightly

This aqueduct at Longdon upon Tern on the defunct Shrewsbury Canal was the prototype for Pontcysyllte and other iron trough aqueducts. It now stands lonely and forlorn in a Shropshire field.

Pontcysyllte Aqueduct near Llangollen is a magnificent structure built in 1805 – the year of the Battle of Trafalgar. Crossing the aqueduct is a memorable experience for walkers and boaters alike.

regarded as one of the wonders of the waterways, it opened in 1805 and is still in immaculate condition.

Chirk Aqueduct crosses the River Ceiriog at the border of England and Wales and is 4 miles south of Pontcysyllte on the same canal. It was completed four years before its illustrious neighbour. At 600 feet long and 70 feet high, it is an imposing structure in its own right, although the later building of an adjacent railway viaduct has robbed it of its visual impact from the valley floor.

A much shorter but still elegant Telford iron aqueduct can be seen where the Shropshire Union Canal crosses the A5 trunk road at Stretton, Staffordshire.

Thomas Telford's iron aqueduct where the Shropshire Union Canal crosses over the A5 trunk road at Stretton. The ends of the aqueduct have elegant curves ending with round stone columns.

Bearley or Edstone Aqueduct on the Stratford-upon-Avon Canal. This 475 feet long aqueduct has a cast-iron trough with a suspended towpath. A series of masonry piers crosses a road and a railway. Not as high or as long as Pontcysyllte, it is still an impressive structure.

Edstone Aqueduct on the Stratford-upon-Avon Canal owes much of its design to the one at Longdon upon Tern. It too is a masonry aqueduct with an iron trough. The towpath is suspended alongside the trough, so the walker gets a duck's eye view of the boats that pass at shoulder height.

At Wolverton on the Grand Union Canal the iron trough aqueduct that spans the Great Ouse replaced an earlier flight of locks. The aqueduct took an inordinate time to build because of embankment collapses and initial bad design.

At Smethwick in the Black Country, the cast-iron Engine Arm Aqueduct carries a canal arm over the Birmingham Main Line Canal. A further example of a canal crossing another canal can be seen at the nearby Stewart Aqueduct, where the Birmingham Old Main Line crosses Telford's later Main Line Canal. Other notable canal over canal aqueducts are at Hazelhurst on the Caldon Canal, where the Leek Branch rises over the branch to Froghall, and at Red Bull near Kidsgrove, where the Trent & Mersey Canal passes under an aqueduct supporting the Macclesfield Canal.

Marple Aqueduct spans the gorge of the River Goyt in the south-eastern outer suburbs of Manchester. The three-arched aqueduct is built in stone and has holes through the spandrels of the supporting arches which assist in weight distribution.

At Marple near Manchester, the Lower Peak Forest Canal crosses the wooded Goyt valley on a massive three-arched stone aqueduct. The engineer Benjamin Outram relieved the weight pressure on the arches by piercing the abutments with holes.

In Wales a stone aqueduct at Vyrnwy carries the Montgomery Canal over the river of the same name and at Brynich near Brecon the Monmouthshire & Brecon Canal spans the River Usk on a stone aqueduct. Both aqueducts are situated in glorious wild countryside.

Scotland has six aqueducts on the Forth & Clyde and Union Canals. High buildings overlook the Kelvin Aqueduct at Maryhill in the centre of Glasgow on the Forth & Clyde. On the Union Canal, the twelve-arched Avon Aqueduct is Scotland's longest and is set in wooded countryside near Linlithgow. The Almond Aqueduct near Broxburn is not as long but is equally impressive while the 500 feet long Slateford Aqueduct is found in the outer suburbs of Edinburgh. The Scott Russell Aqueduct, the fourth aqueduct on the Union Canal, spans the Edinburgh outer ring road. The final Scottish aqueduct spectacularly carries the canal at the top of the Falkirk Wheel.

The widening of the North Circular Road in north-west London led to a drastic reconstruction of the existing aqueduct. The new aqueduct (lower picture) splits into two channels. The upper picture shows the old aqueduct before reconstruction.

New aqueducts are still being constructed because of road building. The Basingstoke Canal now has a large aqueduct at Ash over a new road in the Blackwater valley. At New Bradwell in Milton Keynes the Grand Union Canal crosses a new main road, while on the Paddington Branch in London the Grand Union's North Circular Aqueduct was rebuilt when the road was widened. Another new aqueduct is on the Kennet & Avon Canal at Semington. This was completed over a new bypass for Trowbridge with a minimum of disruption to navigation.

The Drungewick Aqueduct near Loxwood in Surrey has been built to replace a former structure, long since demolished, as part of the restoration of the Wey & Arun Canal.

Locks

Looking suitably festive, a narrow lock at Somerton on the Oxford Canal. Wintry conditions like this may look pretty but they meant extra hard work for the boatmen and their families who had cargoes to deliver.

The basic lock is a rectangular watertight chamber with gates at each end. Paddles built into the gate and in the ground next to the gate are raised or lowered by means of a windlass. This allows water to enter the lock by sluices from above the lock or releases water from inside the lock into the pound below. The gates are usually opened or shut by pushing or pulling a balance beam attached to the gates.

Brindley set the standard for locks at 72 feet long by 7 feet 6 inches wide, which at the time seemed perfectly adequate. This benchmark determined the design and maximum size of boat able to use the locks and became the standard size for most of the Midland canals. The shape gave rise to the name 'narrowboat' for the working boats that used this network of canals. Canals built later, like the Grand Junction, doubled the

Tuel Lane Lock at Sowerby Bridge in West Yorkshire is the deepest lock on the canal system. It replaces two locks that were filled in for road improvements when the Rochdale Canal was derelict in the 1960s. It opened in 1996 at a cost of £3 million and is operated by a resident lock-keeper.

width of their locks so that two narrowboats or one wide barge could pass through. The Leeds & Liverpool Canal has wide locks with a length of 72 feet between Liverpool and Wigan but only 60 feet from Wigan to Leeds, which excludes full-size narrowboats from this 92 mile section. Other canals, like the Caledonian in the Scottish Highlands and the Manchester Ship Canal, have locks large enough to contain sea-going ships.

Diggle Locks on the Huddersfield Narrow Canal are beautifully situated in wild Pennine moorland. This canal was restored to navigation in 2001 after being abandoned in 1944. The waterway is 20 miles long, with seventy-four locks, and is Britain's highest canal.

At Huddersfield a broad canal meets a narrow canal at Apsley Basin, so all cargoes had to be transhipped from barges to narrowboats. On the Leicester Canal the canal company had both financial and water supply problems, so they built narrow-gauged lock flights at Watford and Foxton on what was otherwise a wide waterway. This effectively prevented barges travelling from London on the wide Grand Junction Canal to the broad waterways in the north of England.

The lack of standardisation partly contributed to the decline of the canals. Traffic bottlenecks were common on some of the busiest Midland canals, with boats queuing at lock flights. Narrowboats working in pairs, with a motor boat pulling an unpowered butty boat, were at a disadvantage at narrow locks. With only one boat in a lock at a time possible, the motor boat would have to wait for the butty boat to be manhandled by rope through the lock.

In some places locks are grouped together in lock flights. At Caen Hill at Devizes in Wiltshire the Kennet & Avon Canal has a drop of sixteen wide locks. Each lock has a large adjacent side

Above: *The sixteen locks at Caen Hill, Devizes, became a symbol for all future restoration projects when the Kennet & Avon reopened in 1990. Each lock has a large side pond designed to retain some of the water lost each time these wide locks are emptied. Altogether there are twenty-nine locks in 2¹/₄ miles on the Devizes flight.*

pond constructed to preserve some of the water lost when the locks are used.

The twenty-one Hatton Locks on the Grand Union Canal raise the canal from Warwick towards Birmingham. At Wolverhampton there are twenty-one locks carrying the canal from the countryside to the city centre. The Black Country canals have several fine lock flights. Ryder's Green on the Walsall Canal has eight locks sandwiched between the factories while the eleven locks at Perry Barr on the Tame Valley

Eight locks on the Delph flight carry the Dudley Canal down a steep hillside at Brierley Hill in the Black Country. These locks replaced an original flight of nine locks in 1858.

Eight locks drop the Walsall Canal between the factories at Ryder's Green. The Black Country canals are usually called the BCN (Birmingham Canal Navigations). There were once over 150 miles of canals on the BCN, from which about 100 miles have survived.

Canal have a slightly more open aspect. In central Birmingham there are locks galore, with thirteen at Farmer's Bridge, eight at Aston and six more at Ashted.

Another daunting flight for boaters is the twenty-one locks at Wigan on the Leeds & Liverpool Canal. Flights of locks with a less industrial aspect can be found at Audlem on the Shropshire Union Canal and at Tardebigge on the Worcester & Birmingham Canal.

Staircase locks are built as a single structure, with the top gate of one forming the bottom gate of the next. This type of

A brick octagonal tollhouse overlooks Bratch Locks on the Staffordshire & Worcestershire Canal. Bratch Locks look like staircase locks but in fact a very short pound with side ponds separates them. However, the operating principal for staircase locks applies, as it is impossible for boats to pass each other on the flight.

lock, built to surmount a steep incline, often has an attendant lock-keeper to assist boaters because of possible complications in operating the flight.

Foxton, on the Leicester Canal near Market Harborough, has ten staircase locks grouped into two blocks of five with an intervening passing place. These locks became such a bottleneck that an inclined plane was built in 1900 to bypass the flight. This steam-powered construction cut the boating time from seventy to twelve minutes. Unfortunately it was expensive to operate and was closed within ten years.

Bingley Five Rise Locks on the Leeds & Liverpool Canal raise the canal 60 feet in just a few yards. Even more spectacular is the flight known as 'Neptune's Staircase' at Banavie on the Caledonian Canal; it has eight wide staircase locks. The Caledonian has other lock flights at Fort Augustus and at Inverness. Most of these lock flights attract spectators and several have car parks for visitors.

Cruising times on canals are often measured in lock miles. This is because heavily locked waterways like the Worcester &

Bingley Five-Rise staircase locks on the Leeds & Liverpool Canal. These impressive wide locks lift the canal 60 feet.

Above: *Garston Lock on the Kennet & Avon is a rare example of a turf-sided lock. Only one other (Monkey Marsh) remains of a type of lock once common on this section of the Kennet Navigation.*

Right: *Aldermaston Lock on the Kennet & Avon Canal has an unusual scalloped edge. It was formerly a turf-sided lock, the curved sides being built to withstand water pressure on the edge of the lock.*

Pleasure boating at Long Sandall Lock on what is essentially a commercial waterway. This lock on the South Yorkshire Navigation is electrically operated from the control tower. In its commercial heyday this lock would have passed huge quantities of coal traffic en route to Doncaster Power Station, Rotherham and beyond.

Birmingham take longer to navigate than the lock-free Ashby Canal or the Paddington Canal in London.

In the commercial heyday of the canals it was common for working boatmen to fight over the right to use a lock. Today's pleasure boaters have time to be more relaxed at locks, which have now become meeting places to swap experiences and make new friends.

Tunnels

When confronted with a major obstacle such as a large hill, the canal builders had no alternative but to drill their waterway through it by constructing a tunnel. Even today, building tunnels is a hazardous business, despite the use of modern machinery, as borne out by the difficulties in constructing the Channel Tunnel and the London Underground Jubilee Line. Consider the pioneer canal engineers of the late eighteenth century, who had to dig with pick and shovel and used primitive surveying methods.

In 1766 James Brindley began digging Britain's first major canal tunnel for the Trent & Mersey Canal through Harecastle Hill, a few miles north of Stoke-on-Trent. Geological problems and local mining caused subsidence, flooding and roof collapses. The tunnel was 2880 yards long and took eleven years to complete, by which time Brindley was dead, worn out by overwork and diabetes. Like all early tunnels, it was narrow and had no towpath, so boats had to be 'legged' through. This was a laborious process involving boatmen lying on a plank and propelling the boat by pushing against the tunnel wall with their feet. The tunnel soon became a boating bottleneck until Thomas Telford built an adjacent tunnel with a towpath in

Cookley Tunnel on the Staffordshire & Worcestershire Canal is possibly the oldest canal tunnel still in use today. Although only 65 yards long, it had to be blasted through solid rock. The blue brick portal contrasts well with the surrounding red sandstone rock.

James Brindley built the first long canal tunnel at Harecastle Hill on the Trent & Mersey Canal. Construction began in 1766 but it took eleven years to complete, by which time Brindley was dead. In 1824 Thomas Telford built a parallel tunnel and the two ran side by side for many years. Telford's tunnel is still in use today and the entrance to Brindley's now disused tunnel can be seen on the right of the picture.

1824. The two existed side by side for many years before the original structure collapsed. Telford's tunnel is still used and the entrance to Brindley's disused tunnel is visible alongside. Seepage from underground mine workings has coloured the water bright orange.

At Marsden, the restored Huddersfield Narrow Canal disappears into what looks like a mousehole at the foot of towering Standedge Fell. Standedge Tunnel is 5698 yards long, making it easily the longest canal tunnel in Britain. Once again it has no towpath and one can only imagine the effort required from boatmen 'legging' their boats in total darkness. In later years they suffered from choking smoke and fumes permeating through the ventilation shafts from adjacent railway tunnels. Visitors can take an electric trip boat into the restored tunnel and marvel at this supreme example of early canal engineering.

Dudley is another restored tunnel accessible only by electric boat. It is a very popular excursion for visitors to the Black Country Museum. At 3154 yards, it is the second longest canal tunnel in Britain still in use and has numerous internal branches, including one to a cavern called the Wren's Nest. In 1858 a parallel tunnel was built at Netherton that was wider and had a double towpath lit by gas lamps. Netherton is still used by powered boats although it is no longer illuminated.

Another long Black Country tunnel was Lapal. It connected the Dudley No. 2 Canal to the Worcester & Birmingham Canal at Halesowen. It was extremely narrow and continually suffered from subsidence. The tunnel finally collapsed in 1917, never to reopen, and part of it now lies under the M5 motorway.

The longest tunnel in use by powered boats is Blisworth on the Grand Union Canal near Stoke Bruerne, home of the Canal Museum. At 3076 yards, it is 50 yards longer than Netherton. Although there is no towpath, the tunnel is wide enough for two narrowboats to pass inside. A series of brick ventilation shafts marks the line of the horse-path over the top and these shafts also may funnel rain water on to the boats below. Blisworth had professional 'leggers' for a time during the mid nineteenth century but they were replaced by a steam engine that pulled boats through by a continuous wire hawser.

The Worcester & Birmingham Canal has five tunnels and fifty-eight locks in its 30 mile route to the River Severn. Wast Hill Tunnel at King's Norton at 2726 yards is the fourth longest canal tunnel available to powered craft. There are further substantial tunnels at Edgbaston (Birmingham), Tardebigge and Shortwood (both near Alvechurch) and Dunhampstead.

Tunnels often have wet interiors with dripping roofs and ventilation shafts that can deposit water down the neck of an unwary steerer. These boaters about to enter Preston Brook Tunnel have taken precautions by wearing waterproof clothing.

Most tunnel entrances are prosaic affairs consisting of a hole surrounded by brick or stonework. Occasionally a more interesting tunnel portal can be found, as at Sapperton on the disused Thames & Severn Canal, where the Coates portal has a classical design with pillars and two niches for statues of Father Thames and Sabrina, although there is no record of the statues ever being placed. The eastern portal of Brandwood Tunnel on the Northern Stratford-upon-Avon Canal near King's Norton has a profile of William Shakespeare.

Canal tunnels were still being built in the late twentieth century. Two adjacent tunnels were built in 1974 when a new dual carriageway replaced the narrow road over Telford's Galton Bridge at Smethwick in the Black Country. Instead of constructing two high-arched bridges over the Birmingham Old and New Main Line Canals, the engineers opted to fill in the valley and build a road on top. Two prefabricated concrete tunnels built to carry the canals are called Galton and Summit Tunnels. They looked rather ugly when first built but nature has softened them with greenery.

Another new tunnel is at Tuel Lane, Sowerby Bridge. It reconnected the Calder & Hebble Navigation to the Rochdale Canal in 1996. Even newer is the tunnel under the Roman Antonine Wall and the railway at the top of the Falkirk Wheel in Scotland.

Tardebigge is one of five tunnels on the Worcester & Birmingham Canal.

Waterside buildings

Canals were built to serve industry and very soon this cheap and efficient mode of transport encouraged companies to locate their factories and mills next to the waterway. Many of Britain's towns and cities expanded along the banks of the canal and small communities sometimes joined together to form new towns. In some places mills and warehouses were constructed with their own private loading wharves on an arm off the canal's main line.

With the decline of waterborne trading, companies turned their backs to the canal, preferring to use quicker road transport. Some warehouses and factories were demolished in favour of housing. Fortunately, many old warehouses were spared and have found a new lease of life as offices, flats and museums. The National Waterways Museum at Llanthony Warehouse is housed in one of fourteen brick-built Victorian warehouses scattered around Gloucester Docks. Stoke Bruerne on the Grand Union Canal has become famous for its Canal Museum in a converted corn warehouse.

Shardlow at the eastern end of the Trent & Mersey Canal is an eighteenth-century inland port that has retained several

Cotton bales and coal were once unloaded into the canopied warehouses at Eanam Wharf, Blackburn, by the Leeds & Liverpool Canal. The old buildings have now found a new life as a pub and business centre.

The brick warehouses at Gloucester Docks. Some of these superb buildings became derelict and were in danger of demolition. Fortunately they were saved and are now offices, pubs, restaurants and antique centres. Llanthony Warehouse has become the home of the National Waterways Museum.

The Etruscan Bone and Flint Mill at Etruria by the Trent & Mersey Canal. This mill, which once provided basic raw materials for the pottery industry, is now an industrial museum. It stands next to Etruria Top Lock near the junction with the Caldon Canal.

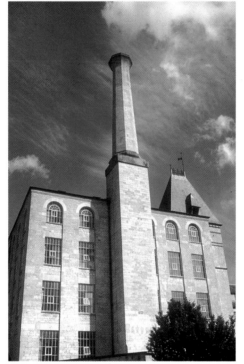

Ebley Mill near Stroud in Gloucestershire. This splendid building, now used as offices, stands next to the Stroudwater Canal, which is being restored.

original buildings. One of these is a splendid corn mill, complete with clock and loading arch, that dates back to 1780. It is now a popular pub and restaurant.

Another superb collection of old warehouses can be seen at Sowerby Bridge, where the Calder & Hebble Navigation meets the restored Rochdale Canal.

At Chorley on the Leeds & Liverpool Canal a former cotton mill has been converted into an antique centre with five floors of art and craft shops. There are similar plans for the surviving warehouses at Burnley, although its finest warehouse burned down at the end of the twentieth century. The fine warehouse built by Thomas Telford at Ellesmere Port on the Shropshire Union Canal suffered a similar fate. Fortunately many of its neighbouring buildings survived and they are now incorporated into the Boat Museum. At Audlem on the Shropshire Union the mill building is now a bookshop and craft centre.

The Adelphi and Clarence Mills at Bollington and the Hovis Mill at Macclesfield are all excellent examples of stone-built mills on the Macclesfield Canal converted to new uses without losing their external appearance.

The Trencherfield Mill by the Leeds & Liverpool Canal at Wigan has the largest working mill engine in Britain and is part of the Wigan Pier 'nostalgia' experience.

When canal companies were faced with a water supply problem, the answer in some cases was to build pumping stations. The most famous pumping station to be seen today is at Crofton on the Kennet & Avon Canal. It includes a Boulton & Watt steam engine, built in 1812, which is the oldest one still working on its original site. The engine can be seen working on selected 'steaming weekends'.

Other pumping stations can be found at Tringford on the Wendover Arm of the Grand Union Canal, at Leawood on the Cromford Canal and at Claverton on the Kennet & Avon near Bath.

The canal companies built lock cottages for their workers, maintenance yards and company offices. One of the finest

The pumping station at Brasshouse Lane, Smethwick, stands between two canals. The upper one is the winding Birmingham Old Main Line and the lower one is Telford's dead straight New Main Line.

Cleveland House at Bath straddles the Kennet & Avon Canal. It was the offices and headquarters of the Kennet & Avon Canal Company.

examples of company offices is Cleveland House at Bath on the Kennet & Avon Canal. It straddles the water at the end of a short tunnel.

Lock cottages, where lock-keepers lived, come in all shapes and sizes. The barrel-roofed cottages on the Stratford-upon-Avon Canal and the round houses on the Thames & Severn Canal in Gloucestershire are among the most distinctive lock cottages. The bridge-keepers' cottages on the Gloucester &

One of the distinctive barrel-roofed lock cottages on the Stratford-upon-Avon Canal. Some of them have had modern extensions added but this one at Lowsonford is in its original form.

Above: *The Roundhouse at Chalford on the Thames & Severn Canal was built as a lengthsman's cottage. The origin of the unusual shape is uncertain but it may be connected to similar structures in the local woollen industry. Five of these cottages have survived although not all in as good condition as this one.*

Left: *The Georgian workshops at Bulbourne near Tring on the Grand Union Canal, where wooden lock gates were built for nearly two hundred years. Unfortunately this production has ended and the future for these splendid buildings is uncertain.*

Sharpness Canal have Doric porticoes, giving them a grand appearance out of all proportion with the size of the dwelling.

Maintenance yards and workshops are a working environment often cluttered with cranes and equipment. Many of them contain fine old buildings like the Georgian workshops at Bulbourne near Tring on the Grand Union Canal, where lock gates were made. The maintenance yard at Hartshill on the Coventry Canal is topped by an ornate clock-tower and is one of the best examples of its type.

Tollhouses were important buildings where a clerk would inspect and weigh a boat's cargo by measuring the water displacement. One of the finest examples is the octagonal tollhouse at Bratch Locks on the Staffordshire & Worcestershire Canal at Wombourne. A neat little tollhouse is one of the few original buildings to survive a huge redevelopment at the former Brentford Dock at the end of the Grand Union Canal. At Little Venice in Paddington the former toll office later served as the headquarters of British Waterways London Region.

Cash's Top Shops at Coventry near the Coventry Canal terminal basin. Weavers lived in the houses in the lower part of the building and worked in the factory on the top floor, which was a continuous workshop from end to end.

A row of stables standing next to Bunbury Staircase Locks on the Shropshire Union Canal.

A canalside brewery at Stone on the Trent & Mersey Canal.

Once a remote boatmen's alehouse, the Globe Inn is now a popular pub by the Grand Union Canal at Linslade.

Before the advent of motorised boats, horses were the motive power on the canals. The provision of stables was very important for resting horses. Most of these have long gone but one or two still remain. The best example is the stables beside Bunbury locks on the Chester section of the Shropshire Union Canal.

Pubs were built by the canals – at first to slake the thirst of the navvies who built the waterways, and later for the boatmen who worked on the water. Many pubs provided stables for the boatmen's horses. Most of these eventually disappeared under car parks and extensions.

The older pubs often had a couple of small bars or in some

The Shroppie Fly at Audlem on the Shropshire Union Canal has a replica section of a narrowboat as a bar. Audlem Mill, which is now a bookshop and craft centre, can be seen behind the pub.

The Navigation Inn at Kilby Bridge on the Leicester section of the Grand Union Canal. This pub by a busy main road has a canalside garden. Waterside pubs like this usually provide food and are a welcome refuge for tired motorists.

cases no bar at all because the landlord dispensed his beer in a jug directly from the cellar. A good example of the latter was the much lamented Bird in Hand at Kent Green on the Macclesfield Canal, where the landlady toiled up and down the cellar steps with her jug full of beer for many years, to the delight of real-ale aficionados.

Some of the waterside pubs remote from land-based habitation would cater almost exclusively for boatmen. A good example is the Anchor Inn at High Offley on the Shropshire Union Canal, which even today is easier to find by canal than by road. Another remote pub is the Black Lion at Consall Forge on the Caldon Canal, where you can watch the occasional steam train pass by as well as the boats.

Today's canalside pubs cater for visitors coming by car as well as by boat. Bars are much more spacious and have extensions for restaurants. Beer gardens often have play areas for children. Some canalside pubs, like the once remote Cross Keys at Penkridge on the Staffordshire & Worcestershire Canal, have been engulfed by housing. Tom Rolt, in his classic book *Narrow Boat* (1944) described the Cross Keys as 'a little lost canal inn standing amid fields beside the towpath'. How things have changed since that book was written!

Into the twenty-first century

The canal scene is never static. In some locations huge changes are taking place, such as the immense redevelopment at Paddington Basin in London, which is one of Europe's biggest urban regeneration schemes. The canalside environment in the centre of Birmingham began changing in the 1970s with the development of Cambrian Wharf at the top of the Farmer's Bridge lock flight. The introduction of Brindley Place, with its shops, waterside restaurants and smart housing combined with the International Convention Centre and the National Indoor Arena, has transformed the entire section between Cambrian Wharf and Gas Street Basin. This former run-down area of derelict factories has become a vibrant meeting place for people in the West Midlands. Similar changes have

Left: *A brand new lock under construction at Moira in Leicestershire. This part of the Ashby Canal is divided from the main navigable canal by a derelict section at Measham. The attraction of the Moira Furnace and its mile or so of already restored canal should help to speed up work on the disused section.*

Below: *A new skew bridge spans a newly restored section of the Wendover Arm at Little Tring in May 2005. The boat in the picture was also new – it was on its maiden voyage!*

Merchant's Bridge is an elegant new footbridge at Castlefield in the heart of Manchester.

occurred at Castlefield in the centre of Manchester, where the Bridgewater and Rochdale Canals meet under a flurry of railway arches.

The Dudley Canal forms an integral part of the Merry Hill Centre at Brierley Hill in the West Midlands. A huge indoor shopping area surrounded by hotels, waterside pubs and restaurants was built on the site of the defunct Round Oak steel works. In Reading the Kennet & Avon Canal passes through the middle of the Oracle Centre, which has cinemas, pubs, restaurants and indoor shopping. A similar development on a smaller scale has transformed the Oxford Canal waterfront at Banbury.

In London a complete transformation of the Brentford transhipment depot at the end of the Grand Union Canal

Narrowboat Way, Blowers Green, Dudley Canal.

Above: *The Kennet & Avon Canal passes through the Oracle Shopping Centre in the middle of Reading. Unfortunately no provision has been made for visiting boats to moor up.*

includes apartments, restaurants, pubs and hotels.

The idea of building new canals would have been unthinkable not long ago but the Ribble Link, opened in 2003, has now connected the Lancaster Canal to the rest of the navigable inland waterway system. There is an ambitious scheme to build a new canal to link Bedford on the River Great Ouse to the Grand Union Canal at Milton Keynes.

Restoration of former derelict canals began in 1964 with the Stratford-upon-Avon Canal, followed by the successful

A new aqueduct under construction at Semington on the Kennet & Avon Canal. It will cross over a new bypass road near Trowbridge in Wiltshire.

The restoration of the Huddersfield Narrow Canal required a new section of waterway to be constructed in Slaithwaite town centre.

The new Drungewick Aqueduct replaces an earlier one over a small river at Loxwood on the Wey & Arun Canal. Along with two locks, the aqueduct has now been completed, opening up a beautiful navigable section in the middle of the still derelict waterway. Trip boats operate on this section from the nearby Onslow Arms pub.

The Anderton Boat Lift near Northwich in Cheshire, built in 1875, connects the Trent & Mersey Canal to the River Weaver 50 feet below. It was closed down in 1983 owing to extreme corrosion. Now restored at a cost of £10 million, it has become a major tourist attraction in the north-west of England.

reopening of the Kennet & Avon and Basingstoke Canals twenty-six years later. The Rochdale and Huddersfield Narrow Canals followed suit at the start of the twenty-first century. The disused Montgomery Canal, the Wey & Arun and the Cotswold Canal have all been partially restored, with short sections reopened for boating.

Metal corrosion caused the Anderton Boat Lift to become potentially dangerous and it was shut down in the early 1980s. At a cost of £10 million, it was successfully restored and

The Falkirk Wheel is the world's first rotating boat lift and a masterpiece of modern engineering. It reconnects two derelict Scottish canals and makes it possible once again to travel from Glasgow to Edinburgh by water.

reopened in 2002. Originally built in 1875, the Anderton Lift connects the Trent & Mersey Canal to the River Weaver 50 feet below.

In Scotland the long derelict Forth & Clyde Canal was reconnected to the equally derelict Edinburgh Union Canal by means of the Falkirk Wheel. Opened in 2002, the Falkirk Wheel is the world's first rotating boat lift and is one of the finest examples of modern engineering anywhere in Europe. It replaces a flight of eleven locks. Two counterbalanced caissons filled with water rotate within the wheel, using gravity to keep the boats level. Only a small amount of electricity is required to get the wheel started.

If the Falkirk Wheel is a wonderful symbol of what can be achieved with modern engineering innovation, the construction of an aqueduct over the new M6 Toll motorway for the still derelict Lichfield Canal is an indication that anything is possible, provided that the money is available.

Further reading

Atterbury, Paul. *Exploring Britain's Canals.* HarperCollinsWillow, 1994.

Bode, Harold. *James Brindley.* Shire, second edition 1980; reprinted 1999.

Burton, Anthony. *The Canal Builders.* M. & M. Baldwin, 1993 (paperback).

Burton, Anthony, and Pratt, Derek. *The Anatomy of Canals – The Early Years.* Tempus, 2001.

Burton, Anthony, and Pratt, Derek. *The Anatomy of Canals – The Mania Years.* Tempus, 2002.

Burton, Anthony, and Pratt, Derek. *The Anatomy of Canals – Decline and Renewal.* Tempus, 2003.

Conder, Tony. *Canal Narrowboats and Barges.* Shire, 2004.

Lansdell, Avril. *Canal Arts and Crafts.* Shire, second edition 2004.

Pearce, Rhoda M. *Thomas Telford.* Shire, second edition 1978; reprinted 2001.

Pratt, Derek. *London's Canals.* Shire, fourth edition 2004.

Ware, Michael. *Canals and Waterways.* Shire (History in Camera series), 1987; reprinted 2003.

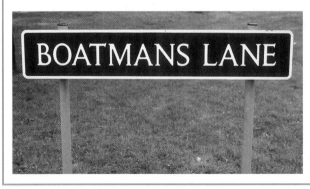

Boatmans Lane, Daw End Canal.

Places to visit

The first number in brackets against the entry is the Ordnance Survey Landranger map; the second number is the National Grid reference. National Grid references are used with permission of the Controller of Her Majesty's Stationery Office.

Aldermaston Wharf, Berkshire (175 / 6067)

Anderton Boat Lift, Lift Lane, Anderton, Northwich, Cheshire CW9 6FW. Telephone: 01606 786777. Website: www.andertonboatlift.co.uk (118 / 6475)

Audlem, Cheshire (127 / 6639)

Barton Swing Aqueduct, Lancashire (109 / 7697)

Bingley Five Rise, West Yorkshire (104 / 1039)

Black Country Living Museum, Tipton Road, Dudley, West Midlands DY1 4SQ. Telephone: 0121 557 9643. Website: www.bclm.co.uk (139 / 9491)

Bratch Locks, Staffordshire (139 / 8693)

Braunston, Northamptonshire (152 / 5366)

Chalford, Gloucestershire (163 / 8902)

Chirk Aqueduct and Tunnel, Wrexham (126 / 2837)

Claverton Pumping Station, Ferry Lane, Claverton, Bath BA2 7BH. Telephone: 01225 483001. Website: www.claverton.org (172 / 7964)

Congleton 'snake bridge', Cheshire (118 / 8662)

Crofton Pumping Station, Crofton, Marlborough, Wiltshire SN8 3DW. Telephone: 01672 870300. Website: www.croftonbeamengines.org (174 / 2662)

Cromford Wharf, Derbyshire (119 / 3056)

The delightfully named Whitsunday Pie Lock on the Chesterfield Canal. It is said that in the 1770s a farmer's wife baked a huge cake to celebrate the opening of the lock on Whit Sunday, but the story may be apocryphal. Research suggests the name existed in the locality before the canal was built. Nevertheless the Retford & Worksop Boat Club holds an annual boat gathering by the lock and a pie is served to the members.

Delph Locks, West Midlands (139 / 8986)

Devizes Locks (Caen Hill), Wiltshire (173 / 9861)

Dundas Aqueduct, Somerset (172 / 7862)

Edstone Aqueduct, Warwickshire (151 / 1660)

Ellesmere Port Boat Museum, South Pier Road, Ellesmere Port, Cheshire CH65 4FW. Telephone: 0151 355 5017. Website: www.boatmuseum.org.uk (117 / 4077)

Falkirk Wheel, Lime Road, Tamfourhill, Falkirk FK1 4RS. Telephone: 01324 619888.
Website: www.thefalkirkwheel.co.uk (65 / 8580)

Foxton Locks, Leicestershire. Foxton Canal Museum, Middle Lock, Gumley Road, Foxton, Leicestershire LE16 7RA. Telephone: 0116 279 2657. Website: www.fipt.org.uk (141 / 6989)

Gloucester Docks. National Waterways Museum, Llanthony Warehouse, Gloucester Docks, Gloucester GL1 2EH. Telephone: 01452 318200. Website: www.nwm.org.uk (162 / 8218)

Great Haywood Junction, Staffordshire (127 / 9922)

Harecastle Tunnel, Staffordshire (118 / 8354)

Hatton Locks, Warwickshire (151 / 2466)

Hazelhurst Junction and Aqueduct, Staffordshire (118 / 9553)

King's Norton Junction, West Midlands (139 / 0579)

Lapworth Locks, Warwickshire (139 / 1870)

Leawood Aqueduct and Pump House, Derbyshire (119 / 3155)

Longdon upon Tern Aqueduct, Shropshire (127 / 6115)

Loxwood, West Sussex (187 / 0630)

Lune Aqueduct, Lancashire (97 / 4863)

Marple Aqueduct and Locks, Cheshire (109 / 9590)

Moira Furnace, Furnace Lane, Moira, Swadlincote, Derbyshire DE12 6AT Telephone: 01283 224667. Website: www.lrmf.org.uk (128 / 3115)

Nantwich, Cheshire (118 / 6352)

Neptune's Staircase, Banavie, Highland (41 / 1177)

Pontcysyllte Aqueduct, Denbighshire (117 / 2742)

Shardlow, Derbyshire. Shardlow Heritage Centre, London Wharf, London Road, Shardlow, Derbyshire DE72 2GA. Telephone: 01332 792489. Website: http://homepages.which.net/~shardlow. heritage (129 / 4430)

Skipton, North Yorkshire (103 / 9952)

Sowerby Bridge, West Yorkshire (104 / 0523)

Standedge Tunnel and Marsden, West Yorkshire (110 / 0412)

Stoke Bruerne and Blisworth Tunnel, Northamptonshire. Stoke Bruerne Canal Museum, Bridge Road, Stoke Bruerne, Towcester NN12 7SE. Telephone: 01604 862229. (152 / 7449)

Stourport, Worcestershire (138 / 8171)

Tyrley Locks, Shropshire (127 / 6832)

Whitsunday Pie Lock, Nottinghamshire (120 / 7282)

Wigan Pier, Wallgate, Wigan, Lancashire WN3 4EU. Telephone: 01942 323666. Website: www.wlct.org/tourism (108 / 5705)

Windmill End and Netherton Tunnel, West Midlands (139 / 9588)

London, Birmingham, Manchester, Liverpool, Sheffield, Leeds, Nottingham, Leicester, Coventry, Bristol, Oxford and Wolverhampton all have canals that are worth visiting.

Index

Page numbers in italic refer to illustrations.

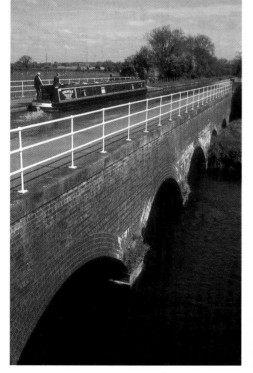

Brindley Bank Aqueduct carries the Trent & Mersey Canal over the River Trent near Rugeley. Colin Dexter's Inspector Morse mystery 'The Wench Is Dead' was based on a notorious murder at this scene in 1839.